Friends
Clare Catford

DARTON·LONGMAN+TODD

To the friends who have held and loved me when I could not hold or love myself.

To those who have journeyed and celebrated my successes, nurtured me through my griefs and who have stuck by me in sickness and in health.

I thank you for your continued kindness, grace and patience.

Clare Catford
November 2010

First published in 2011 by
Darton, Longman and Todd Ltd
1 Spencer Court
140 – 142 Wandsworth High Street
London SW18 4JJ

© 2011 Clare Catford

The right of Clare Catford to be identified as the author of this work has been asserted in accordance with the Copyright, Designs and Patents Act 1998.

ISBN: 978-0-232-52860-2

A catalogue record for this book is available from the British Library.

Phototypeset by Judy Linard
Printed and bound in Great Britain by Thomson Litho, East Kilbride, Scotland

Contents

	Introduction	5
1	*Being your own best mate*	7
2	*You gotta friend*	13
3	*Family friendships*	20
4	*I want to be in your 'gang'*	26
5	*Don't talk to strangers?*	31
6	*Lovers and friends?*	35
7	*Little friends in my life*	40
8	*Old friends*	45
9	*Woman to woman, man to man*	49
10	*Learning to lose friends*	57
11	*In it for the long haul: the joy of long term friendships*	61
	Bibliography	64

Introduction

THE BEST FRIENDSHIPS are kind, warm, intimate, supportive, loving, affectionate, and fun. If they offer so much, why are they often so low on our list of priorities, coming after romantic liaisons and work commitments? Could it be that as I learn to befriend myself, learn to meet my own needs, dare to ask for help, and share my own fears that I will attract and develop more solid friendships and deepen those I may already have? Perhaps this will lead to more loving connections with my parents, my children, my partner or spouse, my neighbours, my work colleagues, my fellow Christian travellers and ultimately with the God of my understanding. Friendship, whatever its shape, whoever it's with and wherever it manifests itself, is a divine gift.

Looking at the story of God's connections with us over the centuries, it seems to me, that this divine friendship is available to us personally whoever we are, and wherever we are in life. 'Ask and it will be given to you: seek and you will find: knock and the door will be opened to you.'[1] I know from my own experience that when I ask for God's support it doesn't always seem to be forthcoming. However, the fact that I have had the humility to ask and put my concerns consciously into the spiritual realm, I believe, means I have ventured into another dimension of possibilities. Asking God to walk alongside me in both good and not-so-good times, also helps me to ask for support and help from my human friends.

[1] Matthew 7:7.

Asking for that kind of back up from our friends, and from God, can be hard. I was brought up to be self-reliant, and initially believed that showing my vulnerability to others was a sign of weakness. Although this 'asking' can be tough to do, it can bring intimacy, acceptance and joy. There is nothing more healing than being able to be 'heard' by a friend when we are at our most vulnerable. By acknowledging that I cannot 'do it' all on my own, I am creating the possibility of a deeper connection, both with my human friends, and with God too. As a result I have begun to see others' love for me often revealed by their kindness and regard. I have begun to discover that friendship and faith go together like best buddies. What follows is an honest exploration born of my own friendship ups and downs, of how to be a friend, both to myself and others, how to keep the friends we have, and how to nurture friendships that may be difficult and challenging.

1
Being your own best mate

I USED TO DISLIKE myself. There were 'bits' of me that I thought were up to scratch, but the messy stuff, the tears and fears, I mostly kept private. If people knew what I *really* was like, they wouldn't love me. Would they? I was never thin enough, pretty enough, clever enough or talented enough. My coping strategy was to be a joker; make 'em laugh, so I could avoid needing to cry. It is often in our earliest years that we learn how to handle difficult emotions. If our parents or carers find it hard to deal with anger, sadness and conflict; then we learn that these feelings are unacceptable. In my family, laughter was allowed, we all have a great sense of humour; but everyone seemed to be frightened of those 'darker' feelings. I hoped that if I ignored the pain inside, then it would disappear. Of course it didn't.

During my student years, I developed an eating disorder; a bizarre form of comfort which later became an addictive way of dealing with all the sadness and anger I felt I could not express. If I let others in on that 'dark' side, it would be too much; I would be too much, and I feared I would be left out in the cold. I eventually told my parents about my illness, and, late at night, I heard them trying to get to grips with this revelation.

'What shall we do? Is it serious? Do we need to call a doctor?'

It took time to understand the roots of this problem, and a long while to let go of the behaviour. I didn't do it on my own. The shame that I wasn't 'normal' was immense. I had a great deal of therapy and counselling, but the real support came from those who shared and understood this illness, both from within and outside the faith community. Finding a support group, where others struggled in the same way, was the beginning of my recovery; and the start of making friends with myself and others.

Being frank with our friends

Honesty and authenticity are supposed to be cornerstones of the Christian experience. It is surprising though, how many of us believe that showing our vulnerabilities and weaknesses to other believers will mean they will reject us, because we may have learned that our faith is meant to make us stronger and comfort us in our tougher moments. Perhaps too, we have been let down by so called friends in the past, which makes it even harder to show our true selves to other people. Our faith may make us stronger, and be of comfort but it can also give us the confidence to show our 'shadow' side too. Jesus was vulnerable, really vulnerable, with those close to him; so we do have a blueprint for sharing those more intimate aspects of ourselves. I recall meeting a woman at an event I was hosting. I spoke honestly about my own struggles with loneliness and depression. She approached me afterwards and wept. 'I have told others in my church about how I feel, how much I struggle and how alone I am, and they told me to pray harder for God's strength. It didn't work.' This is a form of punishment. The implication is that it is our fault we feel such pain, and that somehow, if we prayed more and trusted God more, we wouldn't feel the bad stuff.

When we do not like who we think we are it is very hard to trust our own instincts, and to believe that we can trust others with the deepest longings of our hearts. The wonderfully warm and honest author and theologian, Henri Nouwen, believes, as a result of his own life challenges, that if we can begin to accept our fragility rather than bury it, then we can start to heal and trust others; laying the foundation for nourishing and loving friendships.

Nouwen describes three essential characteristics of the spiritual life. '[Firstly] the connection with the self and the acceptance of your own brokenness, [next] the acceptance of the community and a renewed trust in others; [and] the ability to trust oneself and others clears the path to trusting a creator.'[2] Notice how the connection with the self comes first, before the

[2] Henri J. M. Nouwen, *Reaching Out* (New York, Doubleday & Company, 1975), p. 1.

connection with others and ultimately with God.

Self-regard emerges in Luke when Jesus is asked which commandment is the most important. His response, 'love your neighbour as yourself',[3] although only five words long, underpins all other loving instructions. All the other commandments spring from this. Perhaps the more self-regard we have, the less likely we are to hurt ourselves and others. Cherishing ourselves, I believe, is not selfish, it is essential. Our God celebrates us, despite our failings and limitations.

This might appear to be the opposite of what you and I may have picked up from some received Christian teaching. When I was new to faith, in my late teens, I recall a great deal of talk about self-sacrifice, putting others first, and being unselfish. I realise, looking back, that I was struggling with my own self-worth. Anything that appeared to reinforce the fact that I was not 'good enough' prompted me to sink further into guilt and self-loathing. Although there appears to be a great deal in the bible about a vengeful God and the penalties we might pay for 'disobeying' this kind of divine disciplinarian, all of the 'rules' are set in the context of love. All the 'wrongs' I may have committed, lying, using others in relationships for my own gratification, wounding others with harsh words and actions and so on, hurt 'me' as much as the other. I have discovered that the loving choice for myself, may not be the apparently easy one.

[3] Luke 10:27.

Jesus was constantly faced with difficult decisions, but he managed, with God's help, to be true to himself, say what he thought, and be completely honest despite the consequences. When I look at his life and his death, although I almost grasp the sacrifices he made, he made a choice; he was not *compelled* to hide behind a mask of 'niceness' in order to gain others' approval because he feared they might think him selfish. In a sense, he was truly human. He showed his fears as well as his strengths. Strangely, the more open with others I allow myself to be, the more human I become too, and my friendships deepen and become more nourishing and meaningful.

An example of how loving others can be, when we are prepared to be really honest about our own lives, became obvious when I was asked to administer the wine at communion in my church community. I am divorced; and some of my behaviours, I thought, meant I should not even take communion, never mind give it to other people. When my priest asked me to take on this role, I cried, realising that serving in this way meant that I was forgiven. My priest's wisdom and kindness, had led, in part to my liberation.

Sometimes, even if we don't feel we are worth the effort, it helps to act as if we are own best friend. This does not mean 'making ourselves' do things for the sake of it; if you struggle with depression, for example, often the best thing you can do is rest and take it easy.

However, I have found that by eating well (even when I can't really be bothered) just taking a walk (even when the idea doesn't really appeal) and taking myself to see a play or film (even if all my friends are busy, I can still go out!) helps to reinforce the fact that I am worthy of attention and love … from myself. Saying 'no' is important too. Turning down commitments, whether they are family obligations, work plans or church and community meetings, in the church community, or at work, can be freeing and loving to ourselves.

- Work on your self-regard, asking God to show you how you can value yourself more. It might be that you need some support from a professional counsellor or therapist. This is *not* an admission of failure, but a wonderful gift to yourself.
- When you feel you can, and if you don't do this already; try going to the theatre or cinema alone. Don't wait to be asked. The more you give yourself valuable experiences, the more you will feel valuable.
- Learn to say 'no'. Practice in front of the mirror. If you need an early night, or you take on commitments because you are afraid of being lonely, keep a close eye on the feelings that emerge when you are on your own. It may be that you need to be *more* loving to yourself.

2
You gotta friend

It took a long while, before I made, what I now call, REAL friends. I wasn't exactly 'Billy no-mates', but my friendships were based on being what I thought others wanted me to be. After my divorce, all the friends I had, except one, melted away. I don't believe this was because they didn't care; but when a couple split, after having many mutual connections, the loneliness and isolation that follow can be excruciating. I sat alone in my new rented flat, unpacking boxes, hoping that the phone would ring. It didn't. I had been totally focused on work in my 30s; one boss called me the 'career seeking missile'; I was so proficient at networking but had neglected to make deep friendships outside the office, partly because I did not know how. Work colleagues, supportive though they may be, are not there to provide marital counselling, or hold you when you are in bits after seeing the divorce lawyer. Ironically I had met the friend who stood by me earlier in my career; and her love and support as I stumbled through the aftermath of my split, was unfailing.

I spent time with her and her family some weekends. I began practising honesty; telling her how I was *really* feeling, and not hiding the depth of my sadness. She did not turn away, and I began to learn that I did not have to wear a mask in order to be accepted. Her children were young and trips to the zoo and nature parks, with pushchairs and nappies, were surprisingly nurturing; messing about with play-doh with my friend's three-year-old took my mind off my own struggles. You may find that once you take a risk with someone when you are on your uppers, it may lead to a deepening of that friendship. Recently this close friend has begun to explore her own faith – and she is able to share her deepest joys and sorrows with me. I feel extremely privileged.

Rewarding risks

In the same way that Jesus' followers broke out of their comfort zones in order to be with him, we can take the same kind of action. This can be frightening and we may get knocked back, but I have found that the rewards are well worth it. It was partly out of desperation that I began to try new ways of making friendships. Contrary to what I had believed, it was by letting others see my vulnerabilities that I began to build deeper relationships. I joined a group where others had experienced similar struggles; namely an eating disorder and all the chaos that prompted.

At first I felt panicked by other group members' honest expression of their emotions. Anger, tears and resentment, as well as joy, were all brought into the open. Because this was a 12 Step fellowship for those who wanted to recover from addictions, it was also a spiritual programme. This added element deepened my friendships there, and I was moved by how much love I received from others who had no time for formal religion, yet who displayed acceptance and wisdom.

Joining the 12 Step community felt, in part, like coming home. In the past I had been part of organisations where I really felt I was an outsider. I often thought it was because there was something 'wrong' with me. Looking back, I think I felt this way, because I tried too hard to fit in and lost bits of myself in the process. Just because the people you know may belong to a particular group, or hold particular views, does not mean you have to do the same. This does not make you or them 'wrong', it is just that you may have different needs and yearnings, and listening to those may mean that you decide to go a different way. I had avoided churches after my divorce, and although I am sure I would have made some nurturing connections had I ventured inside a church building, I found very upbeat services out of sync with my own situation.

Each one of us is different in terms of where we feel comfortable and who we feel at ease with. If we think we don't fit in, it is easy to believe it is our fault, but it may just be that it takes time to find our 'tribe'. A wonderful story illustrates this well. Imagine that you are born into a tall blonde family, but you are short and dark. Although you love your relatives, there is always a niggle at the back of your mind that something is not quite right. Whilst travelling the world as an adult, you come across a tribe of short people with dark hair! *Then* you realise what you have been looking for.[4]

It is a fact of life that we connect with some people and not others. If we have a Christian faith we can feel that we 'should' love everyone and anyone. Humanly speaking this is simply not possible. There will be some people we like, and others we cannot stand. I know I have spent too long feeling guilty because I find it difficult to love all people equally. The truth is, if I try too hard to love everyone, I end up loving no one adequately, and simply burn myself out by attempting the impossible. We do not have to become best buddies with those with whom we cannot connect; but if we can *accept* those people as they are, then that is enough. It might be that those people, who we thought had nothing to offer us, end up being close and supportive.

Looking for good mates: what are our motives?

Although it is difficult to admit; I know that I have gone into friendships, because of what *they* might give *me*. I

---

[4] Based on a story by Clarissa Pinkola Estes, *Women Who Run With the Wolves: Contacting The Power Of The Wild Woman* (London, Rider–Ebury Publishing, 1992).

call this seeing others as a commodity. It might have been unconscious, but it is similar to shopping. Without loading on the guilt, how many of us 'shop' for the 'right' kind of friend, in the mistaken belief that they will make us feel better about ourselves because they are 'successful', popular and talented. Jesus' disciples were a dysfunctional lot. Any worldly success they had was left behind as they muddled through their journey alongside the one they had chosen to follow, yet they were the ones he chose to journey with, suffer with, and die for.

Of course it is not 'wrong' to enjoy the company of successful people (whatever that means) or be close friends with those to whom society affords status, but if that is our motive, then we can end up lonely and isolated, our friendships based on superficial encounters.

Jesus surrounded himself with those who he knew, despite their limitations, would be supportive and receptive to him and to his message. He also showed respect to the 'other' as well as expressing 'tough love' towards those who he felt were limiting themselves and others by their behaviour. The Pharisees, and their obsession with legalistic traditions are an example of 'tough love'; he refused to collude with their rigidity and obsession with 'doing the right thing'. He was honest and vulnerable. He was not caught up in pride. A pride that prevented him from asking others, and of course God, for help. My own pride, stopped me asking others for support for years. I was brought up to believe that I should always rely on my own resources, and that asking others for support was a sign of weakness. I have learned that real strength is in vulnerability; in the opening up of myself to others and to the God of my understanding.

For many of us living in the modern world, where relatives are spread far and wide, friends become the new family. This new family though, requires nurturing and commitment. Even if we can only manage a 'phone call or email; staying in touch means the friendship is likely to survive the test of time. I have a wide circle of acquaintances, but a very small group of friends. If I spread myself too thinly, I never have time to move beyond the surface. I hope I am able to support and cherish those friends I have, and I have been moved by their kindness towards me, often when I am in tears and feeling hopeless.

- If you are single, don't rule out families as friends. They can be a wonderful support
- If you are in a relationship single people can add so much to your life. They are often able to still see you as a person, rather than part of a couple or just as a parent.
- If you are normally a private person, or very outgoing on the surface, but find it hard to tell people how you really feel, start to reveal a little of your vulnerability with someone you trust. It does not matter what age they might be. Some of my

good friends are in their 20s, and some in their 70s and beyond.
- Although there will be people you automatically connect with, try and get to know those you wouldn't normally gravitate towards. You may find this very enriching.
- A small group of friends who know you well is worth more than a large group of acquaintances who may only be superficial connections.

3
Family friendships

BIZARRELY, ALTHOUGH WE are *meant* to be close to our families and relatives, this is not always the case. Those adverts that portray a happy couple with 2.2 children, I think, are increasingly out of step with the reality for many of us. In our teenage years, the idea of being 'friends' with our parents may seem something of a fantasy (although I do know people who have had extremely happy and harmonious childhoods). Family dysfunction keeps today's therapists and priests extremely busy. Unravelling painful childhood experiences can often help us lead more healthy lives as adults. But is it possible that we can be 'friends' with those who are biologically close to us, even if the past has not been perfect?

Most parents are 'good enough'. They do the best they can with what they have. You may be a parent yourself, and you will know how tough raising children can be. Caring for kids is a demanding business, emotionally, physically and spiritually. How you parent will, to some extent, mirror how you were raised yourself. For all of us our past inevitably has an impact upon our beliefs about ourselves and about others. One of the joys of my life has been reconnecting with my parents in their later years. My own childhood was materially easy, but emotionally difficult and I needed to work that through in order to be a happier, healthier adult.

It is only in the recent past, that I have really begun to understand my father, and build a real relationship with him. My mother has Parkinson's Disease and is now in full-time care; but during the time she could live at home, my dad was her main carer for ten years. As I tried to support my father, and mother, in this last decade, I began to know both of them at a deeper level. I was able to show emotions that previously I would have been embarrassed to let them see, and they too began to share, in their own way, their vulnerabilities and feelings.

The month after my mother went into the care home I spent time with my father who, of course, was very distressed. I told him I loved him – the first time that I had been able to do so openly – and we both held each other and wept together. Although the circumstances were painful and the emotions deeply held, our relationship was enriched. The more time I spent healing myself from past pain and resentments, the less I expected my father to behave or respond in a certain way. In a sense I took a 'risk'. Because I had been able to show a whole range of emotions to my now precious group of friends, I was able to express myself honestly with my father knowing that if he didn't respond in the way I wanted, it would be hard, but not the end of the world.

Trying too hard to gain your parent's approval is one

way of never receiving it. It's the same with God too. We have God's approval and acceptance already; and when we love the divine and ourselves enough, we want to heal and love and accept others too. God's love is not conditional, it is automatic; however this can be very hard to grasp if we grew up in families where love only seemed to be forthcoming if we behaved in the 'right' way, whatever that was.

Reconnecting with your parents and learning to stop being what you think your family *wants* you to be in order to get their approval and love, and avoiding hiding your real self from your family is, I believe, the way towards true connection with them. It may be, because of their own deep wounding, that our parents and carers were unable to show us the love we, as children, deserved. When we come to adulthood, and are able to see our carers as flawed human beings themselves and not 'magical', then we can perhaps begin to share our own inner struggles. There are also times when it is important to hold back. Telling our families 'everything' about our lives may simply be too much for them, but letting the mask of 'good cheer' slip once in a while has been, for me, a risk worth taking.

Growing up and moving on

The parent/carer–child relationship is a temporary one, in the sense that all adults need to leave their family base to make their own way in the world. This is suggested in Genesis 2:24, although the context is leaving the family for the new permanence of a husband/wife relationship. Nowadays, not everyone leaves home to marry or to become partnered, but the implication is that our relationship with our parents and carers changes as we become mature adults. With our adult status, even if our family finds it hard, we have a right to express our opinions, emotions and spirituality. Even if this promotes conflict, it can also bring deeper connection. My own family has different beliefs to me about all kinds of things. As I have matured I am more than able to hold their differing viewpoints on my faith, without being threatened by them.

Leaving and grieving

It may be that you already have a healthy and open relationship with your parents or carers; if so, that is a wonderful gift. However, if the stories I hear represent the wider world, this is the exception rather than the rule. It is no one's fault. The 'sins' of the fathers are visited upon the children in the sense that all the pain that one generation has, which is not faced or processed, has a tendency to emerge in the next. It may be too, that you need to grieve over the childhood you wanted, but never had. In this context, the words in Numbers, in the Old Testament, are compelling. 'The Lord is slow to anger, abounding in love and forgiving sin ... Yet he does not leave the guilty unpunished ... the children of the third and fourth generation [will bear] the sins of the fathers.'[5] God also promises that this separation (which is how I think of sin) between God and humanity will be reconciled. It is often painful and frequently hard work, but bridges can be built between the old and the young, and these relationships can be nourishing, tender and rewarding. If you are a parent, you were also a child, and so were those who raised you; all generations need nurturing and care in order to flourish. 'A baby is born with a need to be loved – and never outgrows it.'[6]

- Parents and family members are human; the more we face our own difficulties and the more we mature the less we expect our families to be perfect.
- If there is something you need to say to your family and you are fearful of the response, practise saying it to a friend first. We have no control over how other people react, but we can choose how we respond.
- Being open may be painful and may cause conflict, but is never a waste of time.
- God accepts all of us, even our bad bits, and that

---

[5] Numbers 14:18.
[6] Frank A .Clark in Bob Kelly (ed.), *Worth Repeating: More than 5000 Classic and Contemporary Quotes* (Grand Rapids, Michegan, Kregel Publications, 2003)

applies to those in our families too. (Although this is never a justification for abusive behaviour.)

- If we are Christian and our families have different opinions, let them be. We can try to be honest about our spirituality; we can let God do the rest.
- Sometimes we may need to spend time away from our family if there has been abuse or if we receive constant negative messages. This is not selfish, it is self care.

4
I want to be in your 'gang'

'The soul can never be separate; its eternal dream is intimacy and belonging. When we are rejected or excluded, we become deeply wounded'.[7]

IT IS A HUMAN need to want to be part of something. St Paul spent much of his time emphasising the inclusive nature of God's love, speaking to those who were frequently excluded from their own culture. 'Consequently, you are no longer foreigners and aliens, but fellow citizens with God's people and members of God's household.'[8] Being accepted into community appears to be essential if we are to flourish as human beings.

Communities come in all shapes and sizes. Sporting interests (look at the devotion of football fans!), love of music, art, theatre, going down the pub with your mates, and your church community, if you are part of one. This list is by no means definitive, but it shows how much we all love being with other people. Even in contemplation if we pray with others, there is joy in that

---

[7] John O' Donohue, *Eternal Echoes: Exploring Our Hunger To Belong* (London, Bantam Press, 1998) p. 6
[8] Ephesians 2:19.

connection. I recently went on a silent retreat and many of my friends jokingly suggested that I wouldn't be able to keep quiet for five minutes, never mind two days and nights. They were wrong. It was bliss. I sat alongside others, ate with others, had my own personal time, all in silence. Bizarrely I connected with my group, even though we didn't say a word to each other. Simply 'being' alongside others and sharing a mutual experience can be enough.

It is a fact that loneliness is a huge part of our modern human experience. Families are scattered, we move to find work, sometimes to another country, people we have become close to come and go, prompting sadness and grief at their loss.

Belonging blues

It may be, though, that in the past, belonging to a group, or trying to belong has been painful for us. Memories of our school years, where we may have been bullied, when we longed to be accepted, church communities where we feel we cannot really be ourselves for fear of rejection, or so called friendships where we find ourselves compromising our deeply held values or feelings because we worry about what others might think of us, mean that we can compromise ourselves. Many of us, I think, have spent far too long working hard to receive others' approval, partly because we may be unhappy in ourselves. Perhaps we thought if other people loved us, then that would ease the pain?

For me, pride again has been a real obstacle when it came to joining certain groups. When I first went into recovery from addiction I remember thinking, at my first meeting; 'I am not like *these* people, they are ill, they are failures, they can't '*do* life'. Consequently I tried to connect with those who I perceived to be 'successful', and was often very lonely as a result. Many of those I am closest to now, I met at my recovery group. We have a shared understanding of the addictions we struggle with, and a real love for each other based on vulnerability and honesty. This has not happened overnight, and I have had to take a few risks along the way, but it has been deeply rewarding.

Similarly, in my early Christian years, I was extremely dismissive of those who did not share my particular understanding of faith; if they didn't agree with me, then I didn't want to know, due to my own youthful insecurities. My church community now, though by no means perfect, allows me to disagree, share my mistakes and pain, as well as laugh like a drain at the absurdity of our human condition. I have been working for a long time now, towards surrender. Instead of trying to control who I meet and what I do, I trust that if I put myself out there God will give me what I need. Although this may sound idealistic, I can testify to its effectiveness. My day begins with me, on my knees, 'handing over' my life to the God of my understanding. I don't spend hours doing this, or else I get cramp, and it does not guarantee that all will go smoothly, but it does give me a real sense of perspective. When people or communities let me down, which of course they do, as we are all human, I carry on surrendering bit by bit.

> 'As we surrender, we experience our frustration and anger at God, at other people, at ourselves and at life ... Surrender is the process that allows us to move forward. It is how our Higher Power moves us all forward'.[9]

- Take time to find out what kind of communities work for you. Just because you don't feel at ease somewhere, does not mean that there is something wrong with you.
- Ask God for help with this. Literally saying the word 'surrender' sets us up to be more in tune with who we are, and in turn, where will feel most comfortable.
- No community is perfect, and people let us down, as we do too. Look for the similarities and not the differences.
- Be open to new types of people and places; that spirit of openness is very attractive.

---

[9] Melody Beattie, *The Language of Letting Go* (Hazelden Foundation, 1990) p. 302.

- Do not be afraid to admit that you are lonely to people you know will understand. Not every community can cope with this, but those that can are wonderful places to be.

5
Don't talk to strangers?

When I meet someone I feel I cannot stand or I resent (and we all do from time to time), or who I find 'difficult' or strange in some way, I try to delay making a decision about them, just for a moment. I don't always manage this, but when I do, I find the experience enlightening. Jesus taught that we should love the 'other'; and went as far as saying the 'enemy' demands our love as much as the friend. 'Love your enemies and pray for those who persecute you.'[10] At surface level, this seems to be an impossible task, often leaving us with guilt about how we 'should' behave as a human being and/or Christian, and about how we *really* feel inside.

Perhaps this idea can be examined another way? It is often the case, in my own experience, that what I find hard to accept in others is the thing I find hard to acknowledge in myself. So, for example, if someone is outwardly very angry and throws their toys out of their pram (so to speak) and I get angry as a result, might it be that I would like to be angry in public, with no thought for the consequences? As a child I was very compliant, and always 'good'. How I would have liked

---

[10] Matthew 5:44.

to scream and stamp my feet, as I saw others do, but I was fearful that if I behaved that way then I would no longer be loved.

I once interviewed a celebrity who threw a huge tantrum. In a way I envied her, because she seemed to have no fear that others would reject her despite her behaving like a spoiled child. I am not suggesting that we all lose control and behave like brats, but I have found it hard to own and express my anger, and have often been hard on others who can. Our enemies or those who are 'strange' to us may often be people who society deems to be unacceptable. Perhaps the homeless man or woman on the street reminds us that we too could lose everything, but the possibility is too painful to face, so we condemn instead of loving. Judging and scapegoating another is an easy way to distance ourselves from our own feared weaknesses and vulnerabilities. 'Look carefully for those you resent, because they're normally carrying at least some of what you hate, deny or reject within yourself.' [11]

Jesus echoes this in Matthew: 'How can you say to your brother, "let me take the speck of your eye", when all the time there is a plank in your own eye.'[12]

The story of the Good Samaritan shows us how the

---

[11] Richard Rohr with John Feister, *Hope Against Darkness: The Transforming Vision of Saint Francis in an Age of Anxiety* (Cincinnati, Ohio, St Anthony Messenger Press, 2001) p. 170
[12] Matthew 7:5

most 'difficult' people can be a gift in that they make us face parts of ourselves that we'd rather avoid or not acknowledge. The person lying in the gutter reminds us of how human we all are, and how much we can't control, no matter how hard we try, and we walk away, because this realisation is too uncomfortable for us to face – what if *we* were to lose everything, who would love us then? But 'Blessed are the poor in spirit ... Blessed are the meek ....' [13] The beatitudes in Matthew 5 show us how much God values the vulnerable and marginal people in our world.

Joe was a homeless alcoholic who I frequently bumped into on my street. I always seemed to meet him when I was feeling low and miserable; he was kind and accepting, even if he did reek of whisky. I nicknamed him 'my angel' and received much from him. I was not in the business of fixing him; in many ways he was a gift to me. Perhaps we can enter into relationships with people who may have deep rooted problems, and allow them to give to us; this honours them as human beings, rather than always believing that we are 'above' them, and it is our role to 'help' them out of whatever mess they're in. Joe lived in a hostel nearby, and although he may have appreciated the respect and love I afforded him, I think I got more out of knowing him than the other way round.

I discovered later, that life had got too much for him,

[13] Matthew 5.

and he had died alone in his rented flat. I was devastated on hearing this news, but I said a prayer of gratitude for the life he had experienced, and the love he had given me. His critics might say, 'Good riddance, he was a hopeless drunk anyway.' I beg to differ. He was funny and warm, drunk or sober, kind and selfless and I honour his humanity. Without Joe's love in my darker moments, I am not sure I would have made it either.

- When we connect with the vulnerable, perhaps we can consider what we can learn from them.
- When we find someone difficult, perhaps we have more in common than we realise; we simply haven't acknowledged our own shadow.
- Our own personal safety and the safety of our families and friends is always important; valuing ourselves in difficult relationships may mean we have to walk away or lay down clear ground rules.
- Asking God to help us to look at difficult people in a different way is often the first step towards freeing ourselves from our own prejudices and assumptions.

6
Lovers and friends?

I WANT TO JUST put my cards on the table at the start of this chapter. I am not sure I am really qualified to give anyone in a love relationship a great deal of advice. I am now divorced after a 12 year marriage, which ended 13 years ago. However, this does not mean I haven't learned from the experience.

Looking back at my past love relationships I realise that I expected my partners to rescue me, provide for me, look after me and read my mind. What a burden for another human being to bear. I was self-obsessed, yet had no self-confidence. I don't want to shame myself: I could also be loving, kind and supportive, but my own struggles were so immense and my sense of who I was so small, that it is surprising my past relationships lasted as long as they did.

Expecting another to be responsible for our own happiness is understandable, but unfair. Expecting God to be responsible for making us 'feel good' about ourselves and constantly fix us is mistaken too. I have done just that. Wailing and gnashing my teeth as well as bargaining with God. 'Please, can't you just give me a break; all I want is to be *happy*.' God hears and holds all these childlike pleas I am sure, but sometimes I just have to accept that no matter how hard I try, I can't actually control my life. All I can do is make choices along the way, take responsibility for my actions and try not to blame other people for the difficult situations I may have to face.

I cannot, of course, control other people either, and that is profound in a love relationship. I have learned the hard way that to be rigid with and demanding of a partner, expecting them to think like I think, act like I act and believe exactly what I believe pushes them away. And when I behave this way, it is because I am afraid that they will abandon me, and when I act from fear, the chances are what I dread the most will come true.

'We are God's workmanship'[14] is God's statement of love for us in Ephesians. This applies to both people in a love relationship. Admittedly, when your spouse leaves the loo seat up for the sixth time after being asked not to, or buys another pair of shoes that 'she doesn't need', this phrase would not be the first to come to mind. Being friends as well as lovers is important in a relationship; but so is having connections outside the relationship too. Although every romantic comedy going would have us believe that once we have found 'the one', then our lives will be complete, most of us know that however wonderful our partner may be; they cannot be everything to us.

---

[14] Ephesians 2:10

If our partner becomes our God, we are setting ourselves up for disappointment.

Befriending God and Re-friending Others

Through my own pain I have found I have needed to befriend God again and hang on to some of the promises he makes to struggling human beings. 'I will search for the lost and bring back the strays. I will bind up the injured and strengthen the weak';[15] 'I have chosen you, not rejected you'.[16] It is as if, by befriending God in a time of great distress, my real strengths, passions and potential is/are being unearthed. Perhaps this befriending can eventually lead to a re-friending of an ex-partner or spouse, once all the high emotions have died down. Of course this may not be possible for all kinds of reasons, but it is worth considering.

I have recently been on a wonderful retreat aimed at those who are separated or divorced. The grief, the anger and recrimination that often emerge as a relationship ends makes it impossible to believe that things could be different. We all realised, as we sat together, with a box of tissues in the middle of the group, that, in the end, for any partnership to flourish, we needed to take care of

---

[15] Ezekiel 34:16.
[16] Isaiah 41:9.

ourselves, be friends with ourselves, in our relationships. This brings us back to the exploration of self-care in the first chapter – good relationships start with loving ourselves.

One of the things I have found the most challenging in a love relationship, is to ask for what I need. This is particularly hard if you don't know what passions you have, what you really like, and what you really want, so it is important to explore our individual dreams and hopes. Even an intuitive partner cannot read our minds. This also mirrors our relationship with God. The caveat though, is that God knows what we need even if we don't. When I pray, I ask God to give others what they need, not what I think they 'should' have. The same applies to my own life. Sometimes what I need from God is different to my own desires, sometimes it is the same; either way, this 'asking' is a way of letting go which is both frightening and liberating.

Ultimately, human beings seem to thrive in intimate close relationships, be it with partners, friends and God too. This is hard to achieve and means we have to take risks, show our vulnerabilities and be honest. Being friends with our spouse or partner means also respecting them in the way we respect those we care about outside of our primary relationship. By respecting their beliefs, spiritual experiences, their passions and quirks we are accepting them as they are, which, after all is how God accepts us in all our messiness and confusion. We may be 'in love' with our partner, but we are better friends to him or her if we also prioritise being in love with God. 'I have summoned you by name: you are mine ... You are precious in my eyes ... you are precious and honoured in my sight.'.[17]

- Expecting our love partners to meet all our needs is unrealistic. No one can rescue us, we can only rescue ourselves with God's support.
- By exploring our own needs, wants and passions, we are then able to communicate more effectively with our partner. No human being can read our minds.
- Being honest in a relationship is essential. Allowing another to 'see' us as we really are, means taking a huge risk. But if we want intimacy, that is one way to achieve it.
- A shared passion, whatever it might be, means a shared experience, which brings partners closer together.
- Different people express love in different ways; no one does things exactly as we do them.
- Resolving conflict, rather than bearing grudges, deepens any relationship, painful though it might be to do.

---

[17] Isaiah 43:1-4.

7
Little friends in my life

'Hi Clare mommy said that you are making a new book I was wondering if i could be in your book!!!! Me and Oliver are so happy if we can be in your book!!! thanks Henry.' *(Henry, aged 10)*

MY SISTER AND HER family live in America. Henry aged ten and Oliver, who is eight, are my nephews and I love them to bits. When they heard I was writing a book on friendship, Henry emailed me wanting to be part of it, as you can see. I don't get to visit them that often, and I had a few tears when I got his message. It is straightforward, loving and to the point.

Kids don't mess about; they often tell it how it is, and if their thoughts and opinions are heard, respected and acknowledged they will love you forever. Henry's honesty can be near the knuckle. I live in a small flat in London, my sister's home in Boston is much bigger; and I love going there. On one visit Henry piped up with this question: 'Clare, why is your house as big as our study?' My sister was worried that he had said the wrong thing, but it was perfectly accurate, and we still laugh about it now.

I don't have kids myself, and that is sometimes a real sadness. However, I have always made a point of having relationships with children in my life, and it has brought me nothing but joy. There is 'rockin' Phoebe aged one, she has a mind of her own and loves to sing; there is Ronnie, who is two, one of my godchildren, who I don't know as well as I would like, but I hope there will be plenty of time to build a proper relationship with him. Oliver, my nephew, is also a godchild. He is sensitive and funny and he shows me how to build Lego. Oliver was christened recently. We practised and practised his responses (how bizarre to hear 'I renounce evil' coming out of an eight-year-old's mouth), until he was word perfect.

On the day itself there wasn't a dry eye in the church. Henry, his brother, had a stomach bug and nearly threw up in the font; it was difficult not to laugh about that, but he bravely soldiered on. Oliver did us all proud. He had to stand on a box so the priest could bless him and he didn't wobble once. Supporting a child with humour and good grace, without expecting them to be perfect, cements this special relationship; I told him that his christening meant that God wanted to be his friend, and he could decide whether he wanted to be a friend back.

Being childlike before God is not immature. Rather, it shows a willingness to acknowledge that we don't know all the answers and are prepared to ask for help. A child's helplessness, can help us to ask for help; a child's innocence, can help us to let God into those fragile parts of ourselves, that we so often hide.

> 'When you were a child, I loved you ... I myself taught you to walk, I took you in my arms ... I led you with reins of kindness with leading strings of love.'[18]

The quote above refers to God's love for Israel, but perhaps it can also be applied to the rest of us. As a child I loved being caught doing things right, and responded when I felt 'heard' by my mum and dad. I was the creative one in the family, and my mother drove me backwards and forwards from music lessons and my acting club. The most precious thing I received from my parents was time. I would have liked to have spent more quality time with them, particularly my father, but when they were able to simply 'be' with me and my sister, that was worth more than all the music lessons in the world.

No parent is perfect, of course, and no child is either. However, when I hear tales of parents trying to live through their children, or giving a child 'performance love' where their affection is conditional upon how 'well' a child does in exams or sports, I feel sad. These children can spend a whole lifetime trying to please others in the

---

[18] Interpretation of Hosea 11:1-4.

vain hope that they will get the love they never adequately received when they were young. Allowing a child to express anger, and see their parents resolve their own conflicts is a great gift. It means that they are more likely to be able to face conflict in their later life, and become more mature and secure adults.

Being angry at God, raging like small children when life knocks us back, is just part of the conversation we can have with him, or her, depending upon how you see God. I have hit pillows and said 'I (expletive deleted) hate you!'; and I think that God can take it. The Psalms echo this kind of honesty and can offer great insight and healing through difficult times, particularly Psalm 13:

> 'How long Oh Lord? Will you forget me forever ... How long must I wrestle with my thoughts, and every day have sorrow in my heart?'[19]

There is the blueprint for expressing our anger and pain to God, as children, parents and individuals. Although I 'know' intellectually that God's love is unconditional, it would be dishonest of me to say I always believe that; this is a continuing journey for me. As God is simply with us in our lives, simply by being with children, whether they are ours or not is often enough.

[19] Psalm 13 v:1- 2

'Let the little children come to me, and do not hinder them, for the kingdom of God belongs to such as these ... Anyone who will not receive the kingdom of God like a little child will never enter it.'[20]

- Making friends with children means spending time with them and 'hearing' them. It brings great joy and rewards.
- Babysitting for a couple so that they can get some precious time out can be great. You get the child to yourself, decent food, and most of my friends throw in a bottle of wine, although that is not an essential.
- If you're a parent, spending time away from your children, I am convinced, can make you more content and children pick up on that.
- Kids can never fulfil adult dreams, and it is unfair to expect them to do so.
- Childhood is brief (often a relief for parents!) so it is something to be treasured.

---

[20] Luke 18:16-17.

8
Old friends

EIGHTY-THREE-YEAR-OLD Bessie lay in the hospital bed opposite me. I had been admitted after being diagnosed with suspected appendicitis by a stressed doctor. The only bed free was in the geriatric ward. The night I spent there started out in chaos, but ended up being one of the funniest and most thought-provoking 24 hours I have ever experienced. Bessie was wired up to an oxygen cylinder and asked me for a smoke as soon as I slid under my rather grubby bedsheets. 'You got a fag love?' I laughed and politely said no, although being a smoker at the time, I would have loved to have given her a Marlboro Light.

The woman, next to Bessie, was surrounded by loving relatives. She piped up in a wonderful West Indian accent: 'Bessie is a lonely one ... I have tried to tell her about the Lord, as I think he is the only friend she's got.'

The woman next to me was completely confused and kept shouting 'Nurrrrrrse!' in a high-pitched screech throughout the night.

After the relatives had gone, Bessie, the black Christian woman and my 'Nurrrrrrse!' neighbour were left to face the small hours ahead. No one was getting any sleep, and it was a long time until morning tea. Bessie looked very distressed and, as I had been given a dog-eared issue of an ancient *Cosmopolitan* magazine, I went and sat on the chair by her bed. I read out loud what I thought was a totally unsuitable article about which UK locations were the best for making love to your partner. (Well this was *Cosmo*!) When I got to number three, Bessie gave me a toothless smile and said 'Margate!', and gave me a wink. Both of us laughed out loud, and I have never forgotten her wheezing joyfully whilst suffering so much.

A week later, I went back to visit her. She had died. I stood in the middle of the ward with my bunch of flowers openly weeping and a nurse had to sit me down and give me a tea with two sugars. I noticed another elderly woman on her own nearby, and went to chat to her. Because I wanted to, not because I am particularly holy, I began to visit the oldies in that hospital on a regular basis. Ever since this experience, I have loved being around the elderly, spending time with them and hearing their stories. Their company not only eased my own isolation, but taught me much about their compassion and wisdom. I am constantly moved by how much others, who we might not actively choose as friends, have to teach us.

In our modern world, getting older is hardly seen as a blessing. Isolation, poverty, poor health, false teeth, incontinence and loss of skin tone are not, by any stretch of the imagination, dignifying experiences. Yet God sees things a different way.

'Blessed are those who have discovered wisdom, those who have acquired understanding ... she is beyond the price of pearls.' [21]

Pearls, in the material sense, may be pushing it, but being able to pass on the wisdom of a long life lived, has to be worth more than endless shots of Botox to avoid the inevitable. When I visit my own mother in her care home, who, because of her Parkinson's Disease speaks in jumbled up sentences, cries easily and smiles when a song from *The King and I* comes on the radio, I am only too aware of her frailty and vulnerability. My father's devotion to her care is a constant reminder to me of how the elderly are as capable of showing love as the young. By treating my mother with respect and dignity, he shows the kind of regard God expresses to all those who are made in his and her image.

- Old age, reminds us of our own mortality; perhaps that is a blessing in that we come to realise that life is a precious gift.
- Despite the wrinkles (and I have more than enough of my own now) and the false teeth, there is always a person underneath, who needs love, respect and understanding, in the same way that we all do.
- Alzheimer's Disease and Parkinson's Disease are not God-given, and are appalling afflictions. They can

[21] Proverbs 3:13, 15-16

prompt great compassion from relatives and friends, although to watch someone lose their clarity and health is always painful. Perhaps God cries too at the desperation of it all.
- A friendship with an older person is a precious gift, and, as always, I have learned much more from those I have befriended, than the other way around.

9
Woman to woman, man to man

> 'Women supported women in biblical times; women support women today. They care for one another's children, they cook one another's meals [and] they dry one another's tears.'[22]

I could not cope without my female friends. They are there when my love relationships fall apart, they are there to laugh with me and cry with me when life gets too much, and the best friends won't collude or agree with me, if they feel that my actions might hurt me in the long term. However, they do not judge either. I have one close friend who is always brutally honest, incredibly kind, and extremely wise. Our love for each other is mutual. I don't feel I have to wear a mask, or be a 'cheery Christian' when I feel just the opposite, and I think she is able to share her deepest frustrations and joys with me. In my experience, the best female friendships are often based upon a profound emotional connection. A woman will tell her female friend what she 'felt' about her day, and how her emotions linked

[22] Joan Chittister, *Friendship of Women: The Hidden Tradition of the Bible* (New York, Bluebridge, United Tribes Media Inc., 2006) p. 87.

to her experiences, whilst men (and clearly there are many exceptions) are more inclined to share what they 'did' with their mates.

Both sexes, of course, can learn from each other. Conflict doesn't appear to be easy for women, at least it's not for me; but when I have had an argument with a female friend, and managed to resolve it, there is no doubt that our friendship becomes more deep rooted. I travelled to New York, just after 9/11 with my oldest friend, Anne. Whilst out shopping I caught a radio news update as I walked past a cab. Anne didn't hear it. A plane had just crashed in Queens, and everyone was terrified it was another terrorist attack. It was an engine malfunction, but that was not clear when the story broke, and all the New York airports closed, leaving us stranded. When we got back to the hotel, I began filing reports to the BBC in London on our room phone. Because I was monopolising the only phone available (neither of us had mobiles that worked abroad) she couldn't make calls to or receive calls from her husband; and she desperately and understandably wanted to let them know that she was OK.

We had a stand up row about this, and I realised that I was being selfish and obsessive. Eventually she got through to her family, and I apologised for my behaviour. Both of us have never forgotten this, and how we managed to resolve it. We laugh when we think about it now, and as we travelled home on the plane, with a pantomime horse in the spare seat behind us (this was for her kids) we realised how important that row had been for both of us. It is as important as a human being, and particularly as a Christian, to be gracious with our friends, as it is to stand up for ourselves when we feel they have crossed a line.

One of my sister's friends has been seriously ill. The women in her community got together to work out a rota to provide meals for the family to take the pressure off. It was done quietly and without fuss. There is often a thoughtfulness amongst women that is worth treasuring. I had an operation recently, and because I am single there was no partner to pick me up from the hospital. A girlfriend volunteered to take me to and pick me up after treatment. I was so grateful and had been incredibly anxious about how I would manage on my own. The acceptance of women for each other is mirrored in the relationship between Mary of Nazareth (Jesus' mother) and her cousin Elizabeth. Mary was pregnant, unmarried and had been shunned by her community because of her situation. Elizabeth railed against the tradition of the times, and took her into her home, no questions asked.[23] These kinds of friendships are the ones I cherish and celebrate.

---

[23] Paraphrase of excerpt from Joan Chittister: Friendship of Women, p. 54.

Men and best mates

I don't want to pretend that I am fully up to speed on the male psyche. Clearly, I am not a man and generalisations are often far too simplistic. However, emotional literacy, being in touch with feelings, is not often the first thing that comes to mind when I think of them and how they build relationships with others of the same sex. Many, though, have friendships going back decades and are deeply bonded to those they have known for years. They may not necessarily 'talk' about their feelings, but there seems to be a mutual understanding that grows when they share activities together.

Working with men in my professional life has been enlightening. I have noticed that when they argue and fall out with each other, they seem to be able to resolve their differences quickly and not bear grudges. This is not something I have observed in women. I work hard on my own resentments, working out why the conflict has affected me so much, what was my part in it, and what is the payoff for me if I don't try and resolve it. Resentment is a wonderful way of blaming others and staying stuck in pride, as looking at our own part can be too painful.

As women can learn to resolve conflict with each other, perhaps men can also learn to be more open with each other emotionally. The sad tale of the husband who goes into the pub and talks about football with his mates, although he really wants to talk about the fact that his marriage is falling apart, is based on some kind of truth. Younger men seem to be able to share their emotions more freely, so perhaps this is changing. Learning to trust other men without being competitive with them seems to be a challenge. This is not something that is particularly modern. The disciples were often highly competitive with each other for Jesus' attention. In asking whether they were right to tell a man who was driving out demons in Jesus' name to stop because he 'was not one of us'[24] there is that all too human desire for moral superiority over our fellows. Jesus gently corrects their mistaken belief that they are 'special', responding that anyone who works on his behalf is to be honoured.

The disciples were deeply emotionally and practically connected to each other, and, of course, to Jesus himself, and all of them display extremely human character traits. Thomas, who needed to feel Jesus' side before he believed in the resurrection, holds proof above faith; Peter goes fishing even though he is not a natural fisherman and has a tendency to be impulsive.[25] They are all, like us, so human. Their behaviour towards each other ebbs and flows, but Jesus' acceptance of them as they are, soothes their own insecurities and allows them to be vulnerable with each other and those they meet on their journey.

It is dangerous to try and make too many distinctions

---

[24] Mark 9:38.
[25] Paraphrase of Paul Coutinho SJ, *Just As You Are* (Chicago, Loyola Press, 2009) p. 56, based upon John 20: 24 – 29, John 21:3, Luke 5:1-11.

between what makes a 'man' and what makes a 'woman'. Biologically there are differences of course; but I know I can be as competitive and single-minded, as any man, and I also know men who are able to express their emotions and vulnerability, without appearing to be wimps. And perhaps 'wimp' is good if it means showing grace to our neighbours, turning the other cheek in the face of open aggression, and being tender towards your children; something fathers in the past seemed to find very difficult.

When we look at our institutions though, the male influence is still paramount. Corporations, churches, law and medicine are still dominated by men; although I know many women who work and serve in these fields. I have worked in media for many years, and the 'ageing male newsreader, blonde young colleague combo' is still very much in evidence. I often wonder if men in powerful positions actually feel out of touch with other parts of their personality, the more vulnerable bits that they cannot show for fear of being exploited.

Jesus allowed himself to be exploited utterly on the cross, but did not lose any of his inner credibility or strength, though he was sorely tempted to take an easier and more worldly path whilst in the wilderness. Jesus was also authentic. He was authentically vulnerable, authentically truthful and authentically brave because he did not collude with power and status games. While walking on the Sabbath, Jesus' disciples pick some grain and eat it. A number of Pharisees question the action, as it transgresses

Jewish law. They ask why he is part of such unlawful behaviour. Jesus responds: 'Have you never read what David did when he and his companions were hungry? He entered the house of God and ate [sacred] bread.'[26] Jesus is suggesting that some Pharisees are law obsessed to a fault, waiting for Jesus to work on the sacred day and break their rules. Jesus knows what they are thinking and responds: 'I ask you, which is lawful on the Sabbath: to do good or to do evil, to save life or to destroy it?'[27]

Jesus' response is the loving choice; to others, to God and to himself. Perhaps powerful men could examine their own man-made rules and challenge the status quo that says you have to collude with power at the expense of your own integrity. This might lead to the radical step of allowing their vulnerabilities into the open, nurturing their own souls and enriching their lives in the process, and giving permission for other men to do the same.

Both men and women may want to push the boat out, and try new ways of behaving: when I began to do this, the quality of my friendships with both sexes vastly improved.

- Bonding is great, but loneliness is not. By taking risks and sharing something emotional with a female or male friend, you may find a greater intimacy and deepen a friendship.

[26] Luke 6:3-4
[27] Luke 6:9

- No one is suggesting that a man has to cry at the drop of a hat, but bottling up emotions can affect health, family stability, and your own growth as a human being.
- Celebrate the connections you may already have with others. There is nothing wrong with aggression, enthusiasm for sport or for work, provided it is expressed in the right context. By building up a strong network of friends, just a few, when relationships end, jobs come and go and circumstances seem against us, their emotional (and often practical) support can really help.
- Try disagreeing with a boss or work colleague even though it would be easier to keep quiet. You may find you gain rather than lose respect.
- Resolving conflict can be difficult, and everyone has a different way of doing it – but it can bring you much closer together.

10
Learning to lose friends

IT'S A SAD FACT of life, but sometimes we have to let go of certain people in our lives, or they have to let go of us. They may move away, they don't get in touch with us as much, we don't connect with them in the same way any more, or they just seem preoccupied with their own circumstances.

Just after my divorce, when I was emotionally all over the place, I know I became overly-demanding of one particular friend, someone I had known as a student. I remember one awful phone conversation where she said: 'It's always about you; your pain, your marriage split and your feelings; there's never any room for *me*.'

This particular friend had challenges of her own, and neither of us was able to be there for each other as we were both so needy. We parted ways, and this is still sadness I carry with me. Anne, who travelled with me to New York, was able to listen and be there for me, partly because she is extremely loving, and partly because she was in a better place than I.

This is not to criticise the friend who let me go – she had her reasons, and I respect those now. In a way I admire her for taking care of her own needs. Although it felt brutal, she simply didn't have the resources in her life at that time to be there for me.

I have felt the same with certain people. It may sound calculating, but I try to make sure that I balance out people who need a lot of emotional support with others who are not so vulnerable. That said, I know what it is like to be 'needy'; it is no crime, and with the right people, I am able to express that without fear of rejection. Trying to control our friendships is one way of losing them. My experience of surrender, although I still struggle with that, is as applicable when it comes to losing friends as it is to gaining them. As one wise sage puts it; '... life evolves, change is constant. When we try to prevent the forward movement of life, we may succeed for a while, but, inevitably, there is an explosion; the groundswell of life's constant movement, constant change, is too great to resist.'[28]

In my own life, as I come to love myself as my neighbour, and am able to be more open about my needs, and clearer about what behaviour I will and won't accept, I have had to let go of those who don't like me emerging in this way. Sometimes certain 'friends' are not friends at all, they are simply masquerading as such: draining us, contacting us when they need something, and giving nothing back. It is not being loving to ourselves or 'Christian' to give and give until we are wrung out. Saying 'no' is one of the hardest things any of us can do.

---

[28] Jean Vanier, *Becoming Human* (London, Darton, Longman and Todd, 2009) p. 13.

Perhaps one day we will re-connect with those we once loved; perhaps we won't. When I have the awareness to do so, I ask God to bring those people into my life who will teach me what I need to learn and nurture me towards who I am meant to be. It may be that we need to put some distance between ourselves and our family for a while, whilst we get clear about who we are. In my 20s, at the height of my eating disorder, I found it very difficult to visit my own family. I wanted them to love me the way I saw love, and when they were unable to do so, I was left with overwhelming feelings of abandonment.

The reconciliation that took place in my later life, came about, because I stopped trying to control them, and was able to let them be; because I was able to let myself 'be' too. There are deaths and resurrections in all our lives; we let go of someone or something or we are let go, and although uncertainty is incredibly hard to live with, I have discovered that new joys can emerge.

> 'There is a time for everything,
> and a season for every activity under heaven:
> … a time to weep and a time to laugh,
> a time to love and a time to hate,
> a time for war and a time for peace.'[29]

[29] Ecclesiastes 3:1–8

- Losing friends, or being let go as a friend is always painful, there is no 'nice' way to experience it; however it can lead to healthier and more loving connections.
- It may be that, for now, we cannot connect with someone, but if they are meant to come back into our life, they will.
- Surrendering to the God of our understanding when it comes to friendship is hard, but letting those around us 'be' who they are, is the biggest gift we can give another.
- Saying 'no' is hard. Sometimes others don't like it when we change; and sometimes we find it hard when they do too. There are daily small resurrections and deaths in all our lives, as we grieve over a friendship that ends.

11

In it for the long haul: The joy of long term friendships

BEING MIDDLE AGED (a terrible expression, still I console myself with the fact that the forties are the new thirties), I am beginning to reflect on what happens as I get older. I have realised that I rely upon my friends more than ever. They are not an optional extra, but an essential and crucial part of my life. For me, sharing my vulnerabilities, and hearing theirs, whether they are children, my family, the elderly and even those people I find challenging, has allowed me to heal, and become more fully myself

If it is the case that the truth sets us free, then perhaps the biggest risk we can take is to let others into the most painful and private bits of ourselves; we can be truthful about how things 'really' are with others. Sharing pain allows the sharing of great joy too. Being honest with others soothes my soul and brings me ever closer to freedom. Freedom from pretence, from wearing a mask and from others' expectations. For me, the spiritual element of this freedom is profound. As I learn something about God's regard for me, I am able to bring that into all my relationships. As the writer, and lover of deep spiritual practices, Paul Coutinho SJ, expresses it:

> 'I make St Paul's experience my own: in God there are no Jews or Gentiles, slave or free, male or female. I no longer look at you as an object to be used, but I look at you as a person who is loved … I look at you as the breath of God'.[30]

I have just bought the domain name 'growoldwithme.co.uk'. This is an idea for a website, a kind of more mature 'Facebook' if you like, where people can connect for support, a few laughs and practical support as they age. I may never marry or be partnered again (there is no need to weep at this point!) and even if I do I will be part of an ageing population for whom loneliness and isolation may become a reality. This would be an attempt at forming an online community as a way of connecting in an ever-shifting, fast-moving society.

The idea emerged after I heard about some friends who deliberately moved home to be near four of their closest mates. They are a mixture of singles, couples and children. If one of them gets sick, or hits a crisis, the others are near enough to give them practical and loving help. In short, it is a re-creation of community in response to an environment where long term connections are increasingly rare. Growing old with our friends, whether we are partnered or not, can be a rich and satisfying experience; something to cherish and have gratitude for.

---

[30] Paul Coutinho, SJ, *Just As You Are*, p. 149. The above quote is based on Galatians 3:28.

In the process of writing this book; I have come to realise how much I value those I have known for many years; those I have met more recently, and even those who I am yet to meet. Life ebbs and flows, people come and go, and circumstances can alter dramatically. Despite all this, the best friendships can provide sanctuary, support and joy, even amidst the tumult.

I thank God for those who have journeyed alongside me, celebrating my successes, as well as sharing my challenges. They are a divine gift; and my prayer is that I will always treasure them.

> 'Friendship is one of the great spiritual resources of human existence (and) drives us beyond the superficial to the meaningful. It leads us to create relationships that count for something, rather than to simply wander from one casual social affair to another'.[31]

---

[31] Joan Chittister, *Friendship of Women*, p. 16.

Bibliography

Clarissa Pinkola Estes, *Women Who Run With The Wolves: Contacting the Power Of The Wild Woman* (London, Rider – Ebury Publishing, 1992).

Bob Kelly (ed.), *Worth Repeating; More than 5000 Classic and Contemporary Quotes* (Grand Rapids, Michigan, Kregel Publications, 2003).

Henri J. M. Nouwen, *Reaching Out* (New York, Doubleday & Company, 1975).

Joan Chittister, *Friendship of Women: The Hidden Tradition of the Bible.* (New York, Bluebridge, United Tribes Media Inc., 2006).

Jean Vanier, *Becoming Human* (London, Darton, Longman and Todd, 2009).

John O'Donohue. *Eternal Echoes: Exploring Our Hunger to Belong* (London, Bantam Press, 1998).

Melody Beattie, *The Language of Letting Go* (Hazelden Foundation, 1990).

Paul Coutinho SJ, *Just As You Are* (Chicago, Loyola Press, 2009).

Richard Rohr with John Feister, *Hope Against Darkness: The Transforming Vision of Saint Francis in an Age of Anxiety* (Cincinnati, Ohio, St Anthony Messenger Press, 2001).